22 60

OCT   2001

D161180

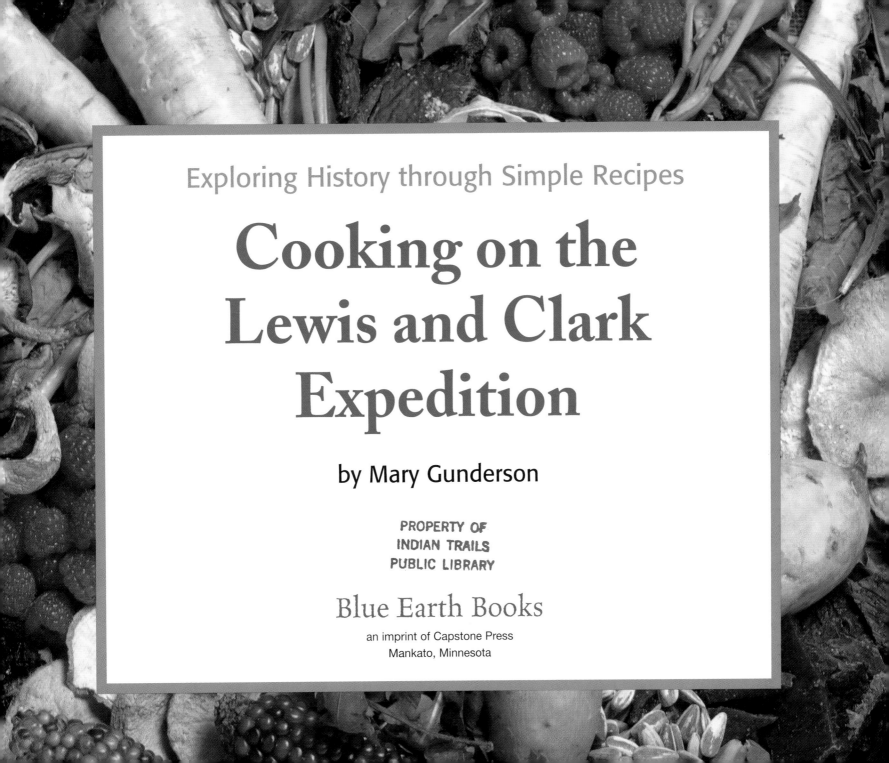

Exploring History through Simple Recipes

Cooking on the Lewis and Clark Expedition

by Mary Gunderson

Blue Earth Books

an imprint of Capstone Press
Mankato, Minnesota

Blue Earth Books are published by Capstone Press
151 Good Counsel Drive, P.O. Box 669, Mankato, Minnesota 56002
http://www.capstone-press.com

Library of Congress Cataloging-in-Publication Data
Gunderson, Mary.
    Cooking on the Lewis and Clark Expedition / by Mary Gunderson.
    p. cm.—(Exploring history through simple recipes)
    Includes bibliographical references (p. 30) and index.
    Summary: Discusses the everyday life, cooking methods, and foods eaten on the journey of Meriwether Lewis and William Clark up and beyond
the Missouri River to the Pacific as they charted the vast territory of the Louisiana Purchase. Includes recipes.
    ISBN 0-7368-0354-8
    1. Cookery, American—Western style—History Juvenile literature. 2. Food habits—West (U.S.)—History—19th century Juvenile literature.
3. Lewis and Clark Expedition (1804-1806). Juvenile literature. [1. Cookery, American—Western style—History. 2. Food habits—West (U.S.)—
History—19th century. 3. Lewis and Clark Expedition (1804-1806). 4. Frontier and pioneer life—West (U.S.).] I. Title. II. Series.
TX715.2.W47G86   2000
641.5978'09034—dc21
                                                                                                                                99-24614
                                                                                                                                CIP

Editorial credits
Editors, Rebecca Glaser, Rachel Koestler; cover designer, Steve
Christensen; interior designer, Heather Kindseth; illustrator, Linda
Clavel; photo researcher, Kimberly Danger; historical consultant: Sally
Freeman, Fort Clatsop National Memorial Park Ranger.

Acknowledgments
Blue Earth Books thanks the following children who helped test recipes:
John Christensen, Matthew Christensen, Maerin Coughlan, Beth
Goebel, Nicole Hilger, Abby Rothenbuehler, Alice Ruff, Hannah
Schoof, and Molly Wandersee.

The author thanks Lisa Golden Schroeder for her research assistance.

1 2 3 4 5 6 05 04 03 02 01 00

Photo credits
Corbis-Bettmann, cover; Gregg Andersen, cover (background) and
recipes, 17, 19, 23, 25; The Beinecke Rare Book and Manuscript Library,
Yale University, 6, 10; Charles Willson Peale Independence National
Historical Park, 8, 9; Oregon Historical Society Photographic Dept., 13;
Morgan Williams, Viesti Associates, Inc., 14-15; North Wind Picture
Archives, 16, 17, 21; Wyoming Division of Cultural Resources, 18;
Joslyn Art Museum, Omaha, Nebraska, 22; Wm. Munoz, 26;
Dembinsky Photo Assoc., 24; Smithsonian Institution, Photographic
Services, 27; Archive Photos, 28.

Editor's note
Adult supervision may be needed for some recipes in this book. All
recipes have been tested. Although based on historical foods, recipes
have been modernized and simplified for today's young cooks.

Contents

Cooking Help

Recipes

References

Metric Conversion Guide

U.S.	Canada
¼ teaspoon	1 mL
½ teaspoon	2 mL
1 teaspoon	5 mL
1 tablespoon	15 mL
¼ cup	50 mL
⅓ cup	75 mL
½ cup	125 mL
⅔ cup	150 mL
¾ cup	175 mL
1 cup	250 mL
1 quart	1 liter
1 ounce	30 grams
2 ounces	55 grams
4 ounces	85 grams
½ pound	225 grams
1 pound	455 grams

Fahrenheit	Celsius
325 degrees	160 degrees
350 degrees	180 degrees
375 degrees	190 degrees
400 degrees	200 degrees
425 degrees	220 degrees

Kitchen Safety

1. Make sure your hair and clothes will not be in the way while you are cooking.

2. Keep a fire extinguisher in the kitchen. Never put water on a grease fire.

3. Wash your hands with soap before you start to cook. Wash your hands with soap again after you handle meat or poultry.

4. Ask an adult for help with sharp knives, the stove, the oven, and all electrical appliances.

5. Turn handles of pots and pans to the middle of the stove. A person walking by could run into handles that stick out toward the room.

6. Use dry pot holders to take dishes out of the oven.

7. Wash all fruits and vegetables.

8. Always use a clean cutting board. Wash the cutting board thoroughly after cutting meat or poultry.

9. Wipe up spills immediately.

10. Store leftovers properly. Do not leave leftovers out at room temperature for more than two hours.

Cooking Equipment

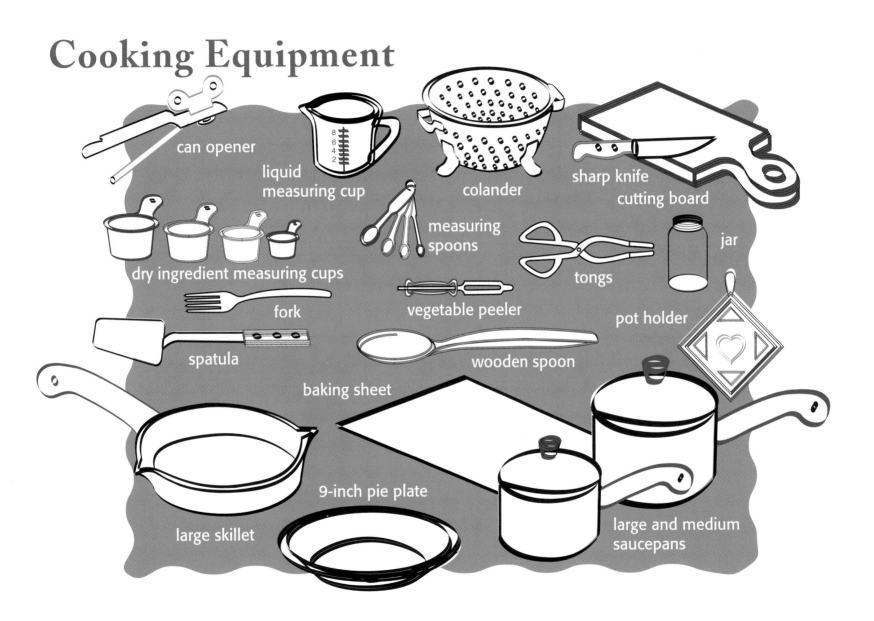

can opener

liquid measuring cup

colander

sharp knife

cutting board

measuring spoons

jar

dry ingredient measuring cups

tongs

fork

vegetable peeler

pot holder

spatula

wooden spoon

baking sheet

9-inch pie plate

large skillet

large and medium saucepans

The Lewis and Clark Expedition

In 1803, the United States purchased the Louisiana Territory from France for $15 million. This area of land stretched from the Mississippi River to the Rocky Mountains and from the Gulf of Mexico to the Canadian border. The Louisiana Purchase doubled the size of the United States.

President Thomas Jefferson and his secretary, Meriwether Lewis, planned an expedition to the Louisiana Territory. Jefferson wanted Lewis to search for a river route from the Mississippi River to the Pacific Ocean. At that time, many people believed there was such a Northwest Passage. A river route connecting the Atlantic Ocean to the Pacific Ocean would help the United States transport goods and increase trade with Asian countries.

Lewis asked his friend William Clark to help plan and lead the expedition. Lewis and Clark formed a team called the Corps of Discovery. This group of about 45 men planned to travel mostly by boat. The Corps of Discovery included men who were soldiers, blacksmiths, and French fur trappers. Clark's African American slave, York, also traveled with the Corps. Lewis brought along his Newfoundland dog, Seaman.

From 1804 to 1806, members of the expedition explored the western United States. The group left from a spot near St. Louis in 1804 and followed the Missouri River northwest to what is now North Dakota. They then headed west to explore the area of the present-day states of Montana, Idaho, Washington, and Oregon. The Corps of Discovery reached the Pacific Ocean on November 15, 1805. Lewis and Clark each took a separate route for part of the return journey to explore more land in this territory.

Handmade maps and drawings record the expedition. These preserved documents give us a first-hand look at history.

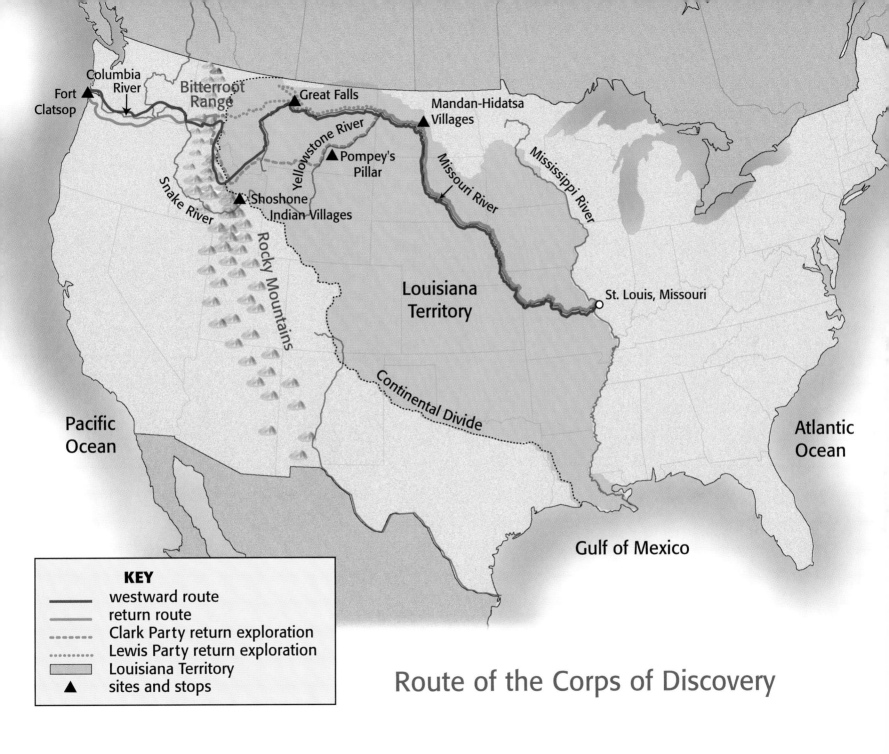

Columbia River

Fort Clatsop

Bitterroot Range

Great Falls

Mandan-Hidatsa Villages

Yellowstone River

Pompey's Pillar

Missouri River

Mississippi River

Snake River

Shoshone Indian Villages

Rocky Mountains

Louisiana Territory

St. Louis, Missouri

Pacific Ocean

Continental Divide

Atlantic Ocean

Gulf of Mexico

KEY

—— westward route
—— return route
----- Clark Party return exploration
······ Lewis Party return exploration
▢ Louisiana Territory
▲ sites and stops

Route of the Corps of Discovery

Meriwether Lewis (1774-1809)

Meriwether Lewis was born and raised in Virginia. His family and Thomas Jefferson's family were neighbors. Lewis attended school for five years, which was more than most people at the time. He wanted to go to college, but he stayed home to take care of the family farm.

Lewis joined the U.S. Army when he was 20 years old. He served as a soldier on the frontier of western Ohio, where he met William Clark. The army promoted Lewis to the rank of captain after he had served for six years.

In 1801, Jefferson appointed Lewis as his personal secretary. Lewis traveled and attended meetings with Jefferson. Jefferson wanted someone he could trust to lead the exploration of the West. To help Lewis prepare for the expedition, Jefferson taught him about navigation and mapmaking. Later, Lewis traveled to Philadelphia to learn more about biology, astronomy, mapmaking, and medicine. He also learned what was known about the western frontier at the time.

After the expedition, Jefferson rewarded Lewis by appointing him the governor of the Territory of Upper Louisiana. This job was challenging for Lewis. He was not good at resolving conflicts between the American Indians and the business interests of the United States. Lewis planned a trip to Washington, D.C., to meet with Jefferson. Lewis died while he was on this trip.

William Clark (1770–1838)

William Clark was born in Virginia in 1770. He was the ninth of 10 children. He grew up in what is now Kentucky. In Clark's time, few white people had settled this area. Clark spent much of his time exploring the land near his family's home. Clark received a little schooling from his older brothers.

Clark joined the Kentucky Militia in 1789. He later joined the U.S. Army. Clark built forts during his time in the army. He fought against American Indian groups and led groups of soldiers through dangerous territory. Clark's experiences in the army prepared him to help Meriwether Lewis lead the expedition to the West.

After the expedition, Clark married Julia Hancock of Virginia. They named their first son Meriwether Lewis Clark, in honor of Lewis. The Clarks had four more children. Julia died in 1820. Clark married Harriet Radford the next year. They had two children.

Clark had a successful career after the expedition. Jefferson appointed him as an American Indian agent for the Louisiana Territory. He was a representative to American Indian groups, many of which he had met on the expedition. In 1813, President James Madison named Clark as the governor of the newly formed Missouri Territory. In 1822, Clark became the Superintendent of Indian Affairs as a representative to all American Indian groups in the United States. Clark died in 1838.

Planning for the Expedition

Lewis was in charge of buying all the supplies the Corps would carry on the expedition. He planned to spend $2,500 for expedition preparations. Instead, Lewis needed $38,000 to fund the expedition. President Jefferson made sure all the bills were paid.

Lewis shopped for food before the trip. He bought 3,400 pounds (1,542 kilograms) of flour, 3,705 pounds (1,681 kilograms) of pork, and 1,000 pounds (450 kilograms) of hominy, or hulled corn. Lewis ordered 193 pounds (87 kilograms) of portable soup. The men could mix this dried or pastelike mixture with hot water to make soup.

Lewis knew that some of the food might spoil. He bought salt, cinnamon, pepper, and red pepper. The Corps members could add these spices to spoiled food to make it taste better.

Lewis bought plenty of hunting and fishing equipment. The men counted on being able to hunt and fish for food during the journey. Lewis packed extra parts to repair rifles. He bought gunpowder packed in 52 lead canisters. The men could later melt down the canisters to make bullets. Lewis also packed a supply of fishing line and 2,800 fishhooks that also were valuable as trade goods.

Each man had a gun, a knife, and two packs. One pack held his blanket, personal items, and eating utensils. The other pack held bullets and gunpowder. In this pack, each man also carried a spoon and a tin cup with no handle, called a corn boiler. The explorers used the corn boiler as a bowl for food and as a cup for coffee, soup, or whiskey.

Lewis brought gifts for American Indians, including beads, pots, cloth, pipes, and silver peace medals. The gifts were meant to show American Indians that the United States was a wealthy nation and that the explorers meant no harm.

A copy of the list Lewis made for the expedition includes supplies such as coffee, pork, beans, peas, flour, and cornmeal.

Hominy and Bacon

Hominy is made from kernels of corn soaked in lye and then washed to remove the hulls. Look for canned hominy in supermarkets.

Ingredients
4 strips bacon
1 medium onion
1 can (15.5 ounces) white
 or yellow hominy
⅛ teaspoon salt
⅛ teaspoon ground black pepper

Equipment
cutting board
sharp knife
dry-ingredient measuring cups
large skillet or electric skillet
empty can or glass jar
measuring spoons
wooden spoon
tongs
paper towel
can opener
colander

1. Cut four strips of bacon into ½-inch (1.3-centimeter) pieces.
2. Cook bacon over medium heat until almost crisp.
3. Place bacon on paper towel to cool.
4. Carefully pour bacon fat into an empty can or jar. Spoon 1 tablespoon fat back into skillet.
5. Remove peel from onion. Chop onion. Measure ½ cup chopped onion.
6. Cook onion over medium heat in bacon fat until tender.
7. Open can of hominy and drain liquid.
8. Add hominy, bacon, ⅛ teaspoon salt, and ⅛ teaspoon pepper to onion. Stir.
9. Cook 5 minutes, stirring occasionally, until hot.

Makes 6 servings

First Days on the Lower Missouri River

On May 14, 1804, the Corps of Discovery began the expedition at Camp Wood River, north of St. Louis, on the Mississippi River. They crossed the Mississippi River and entered the mouth of the Missouri River. They then traveled north through what is now Missouri and along what is now the Iowa-Nebraska border. This section of the lower Missouri River was well-traveled. American Indians lived along the riverbanks.

Lewis arranged for three boats to carry the men and their supplies. The group would use a 55-foot (17-meter) long keelboat with a flat bottom to navigate the sometimes shallow Missouri River. Two large canoe-shaped boats called pirogues carried the remaining load.

Lewis and Clark divided the Corps into groups called messes to cook and eat. Members of each mess cooked the main meal of the day when they stopped at night. The men did not take time to cook during the day. They saved some food from the evening meal for the next day's breakfast and lunch.

John Ordway, one of the sergeants on the expedition, issued food rations in a three-day cycle set up by Lewis.

On day one, he issued hominy and lard. Members of the Corps received salt pork and flour on day two. On day three, the men received cornmeal and pork. The cycle then repeated. To conserve food, Lewis also ordered that

> "...in a fiew minits Cought three verry large Catfish one nearly white, Those fish are in great plenty on the Sides of the river and verry fat, a quart of Oile Came out of the Surpolous fat of one of these fish..."
>
> William Clark, July 29th, 1804

"no poark [pork] is to be issued when we have fresh meat on hand."

George Droulliard was the main hunter of the expedition. He and two or three other men hunted every day. They often killed a deer or a bear.

The Corps also fished for catfish. Catfish were large and plentiful in the Missouri River. To catch the fish, the explorers cut a tree branch to use as a pole. They tied a fishing line with a hook to the tree branch. The men fried the fish they caught in a pan or roasted fish on sticks over the fire.

Silver Peace Medals

Lewis and Clark brought many gifts for the American Indian groups they would meet. Silver peace medals were one such gift. The medals showed an American Indian's hand and a white man's hand clasped together. On the other side, is a likeness of President Thomas Jefferson. Lewis and Clark usually gave these medals to chiefs and other high-ranking members of American Indian groups.

Jefferson wanted Lewis and Clark to impress any American Indian groups they met. Lewis also brought beads, tomahawks, axes, mirrors, and tobacco. These items showed the American Indians the riches that white people could offer.

Pan-fried Catfish

Farm-raised catfish fillets are available in the frozen foods section of the supermarket.

Ingredients
⅓ cup yellow cornmeal
¼ teaspoon salt
¼ teaspoon ground black pepper
3 catfish fillets (about 8 ounces each)
2 tablespoons vegetable oil

Equipment
9-inch pie plate
dry-ingredient measuring cups
measuring spoons
medium skillet or electric skillet
spatula
fork

1. In pie plate, combine ⅓ cup cornmeal, ¼ teaspoon salt, and ¼ teaspoon pepper.
2. Place fish fillets one at a time in cornmeal mixture. Turn to completely coat both sides. Repeat with remaining fillets.
3. Heat oil in skillet over medium-high heat about 1 minute.
4. Add catfish. Reduce heat to medium. Cook 3 to 4 minutes.
5. Turn catfish. Cook 3 to 4 minutes or until fish is golden brown and flakes easily with fork.

Makes 6 servings.

Buffalo and the Middle Missouri River

The Corps saw their first herds of buffalo in August of 1804, after they reached the middle Missouri River. This part of the river starts near where the present-day states of Iowa, Nebraska, and South Dakota meet. The river then stretches northwest into what is now North Dakota. As many as 60 million buffalo lived on the plains of the Louisiana Territory. More buffalo than people lived in North America at that time.

The Lakota, Mandan, Hidatsa, and other American Indians who lived on the Great Plains hunted the buffalo. American Indians used buffalo skins to cover tepees, line boats, and make clothing. They carved utensils out of buffalo bones. They ate buffalo meat fresh, roasted, dried, boiled, and stewed.

The explorers hunted buffalo for food as often as possible. When buffalo was plentiful, each man ate up to 9 pounds (4 kilograms) of meat per day. Lewis reported that the roasted hump was especially delicious.

The explorers ate a great deal of buffalo jerky. To make the jerky, they coated strips of fresh meat with salt and other spices. They threaded the meat on sticks to dry over the campfire. The meat cooked and became chewy as the moisture in the meat evaporated overnight. If the meat was not dry in the morning, the explorers tied the strips to the keelboat mast to finish drying as they traveled.

Buffalo or Beef Jerky

Plan on one hour pre-preparation time for this recipe. Store jerky in refrigerator.

Ingredients
1 pound buffalo* or very lean beef
1 tablespoon salt
½ teaspoon ground black pepper

Equipment
cutting board
sharp knife
measuring spoons
large sealable plastic bag
 or plastic bag with twist tie
jelly roll pan
aluminum foil
wire baking rack
pot holders
tongs

Millions of buffalo grazed on the grasslands of the Great Plains in the early 1800s. But by 1895, settlers and soldiers had killed so many buffalo that only about 800 wild buffalo still survived in the United States.

1. Partially freeze meat for 20 minutes to 1 hour to make slicing easier.
2. Preheat oven to 175°F (90°C).
3. Cut meat diagonally across the grain so that each piece is 6 inches (15 centimeters) long, 3 inches (8 centimeters) wide, and ⅛ to ¼ inches (3 to 6 millimeters) thick.
4. Cut away remaining fat.
5. Place meat strips, 1 tablespoon salt, and ½ teaspoon pepper in plastic bag. Seal tightly. Shake bag to coat meat with seasoning.
6. Line the bottom of jelly roll pan with a sheet of aluminum foil. Place wire baking rack on top of the pan.
7. Remove meat strips from bag. Lay strips of meat on wire baking rack. Place pan on middle rack of oven. Leave oven door open a crack for moisture to escape.
8. Bake 4 to 5 hours or until meat is dry but still slightly chewy.

*Available in some supermarkets and by special order.

15

Fort Mandan

On October 24, 1804, the Lewis and Clark expedition reached its first goal. The men planned to spend the winter at the Mandan-Hidatsa villages in what is now central North Dakota. These American Indian villages were the main trading center on the Northern Plains.

The Mandans and Hidatsas allowed the explorers to build a small fort. The explorers named it Fort Mandan. They lived there for five months through a cold, snowy winter. The members of the Corps spent their days hunting, socializing, and trading with the villagers.

Mandan and Hidatsa women were expert farmers. They grew many varieties of corn, squash, and beans for soups and stews. They picked wild Juneberries and sand cherries for sauces. The Mandan and Hidasta women mixed chokecherries with hot water for medicine. They dried fruits and vegetables to use during the winter.

The Corps of Discovery gathered supplies for the next part of the journey. They

This Mandan earth lodge has been reconstructed and can be seen at On-A-Slant Indian Village on the Missouri River in North Dakota.

A reconstructed Fort Mandan stands at the Lewis and Clark site on the Missouri River in North Dakota.

traded beads, axe blades, cloth, and pots with the Mandans and Hidatsas in exchange for food.

In March 1805, the travelers began packing to leave their winter camp. After the ice melted, Lewis sent the keelboat and about 16 men back to St. Louis. They carried back reports and samples of plants and animals.

On April 8, 1805, a reassembled Corps of 33 people and Lewis's dog, Seaman, left the villages. The men had carved six new canoes from large cottonwood trees. The group traveled in these canoes and the two pirogues.

Cherry Sauce

The Mandans and Hidatsas would have used dried cherries to make this type of sauce.

Ingredients
2 cups water
¼ cup all-purpose flour
2 tablespoons honey or granulated sugar
⅛ teaspoon salt
3 cups dark, sweet, pitted cherries (canned or frozen)

Equipment
medium saucepan
liquid measuring cup
dry-ingredient measuring cups
measuring spoons
wooden spoon

1. In saucepan, combine 2 cups water, ¼ cup flour, 2 tablespoons honey, and ⅛ teaspoon salt. Stir to mix well.
2. Stir in 3 cups cherries. Bring mixture to a boil.
3. Reduce heat to low. Cook, stirring frequently, until mixture is thickened and bubbly.
   Serve hot as a dessert topping.

Makes 6 to 7 servings

17

Sacagawea and Her Family

A family from the Mandan and Hidatsa villages joined the Corps. French trapper and trader Toussaint Charbonneau (too-SAHNT SHAR-bahn-no) agreed to help the explorers. He brought his young wife, Sacagawea (sah-KAH-gah-wee-a), and their two-month-old baby, Jean Baptiste. Sacagawea was a Shoshone Indian. She could translate for the Corps when they met Shoshones in the days ahead.

Sacagawea was important to the expedition in other ways. American Indian groups understood that a woman and baby's presence with the Corps meant the group was peaceful.

Sacagawea, Charbonneau, and several of the soldiers once were caught in a sudden windstorm in their boat. Charbonneau panicked while Sacagawea remained calm. She quickly reached for journals, maps, and instruments that started to float away. These items were very important to the work of Lewis and Clark. Lewis had watched the accident from shore. He noted in his journal: "The Indian woman, to whom I ascribe equal fortitude and resolution with any person on board at the time of the accedent, caught and preserved most of the light articles, which were washed overboard."

Sacagawea gathered wild licorice, currants, and wild roots to eat during the expedition. On April 9, 1805, Lewis reported "when we halted for dinner the squaw busied herself in searching for the wild artichokes which the mice collect and deposit in large hoards…her labour soon proved successful, and she procured a good quantity of these roots." Lewis described the roots as similar to Jerusalem artichokes in flavor, but smaller in size. The men cooked the roots in the ashes of the campfire. The roots tasted like potatoes with a nutty flavor. The Corps members ate the cooked roots with parched corn and buffalo jerky.

Roasted Jerusalem Artichokes

Look for Jerusalem artichokes in the produce department. They sometimes are called sunchokes.

This statue in Bismarck, North Dakota, shows Sacagawea as she may have looked when she helped the expedition. Wild roots like Jerusalem artichokes were among the foods she showed members of the expedition how to find, cook, and eat.

Ingredients
1 pound (6-8) Jerusalem artichokes
1 tablespoon butter or margarine
⅛ teaspoon salt
⅛ teaspoon ground black pepper

Equipment
cutting board
sharp knife or potato peeler
aluminum foil, 10-inch by 6-inch
   (25-centimeter by 15-centimeter)
measuring spoons
baking sheet

1. Preheat oven to 400° F.
2. Wash and thinly peel the artichokes. Cut them in half.
3. Place on 10-inch by 6-inch (25-centimeter by 15-centimeter) piece of aluminum foil.
4. Dot with butter.
5. Sprinkle with salt and pepper.
6. Bring sides of foil together and fold so foil is sealed. Place on baking sheet.
7. Bake about 50 minutes, or until artichokes are tender enough to be easily speared with a fork.

Serve as a side dish.   Makes 6 to 8 servings.

In June 1805, the Corps reached the Great Falls on the Missouri River in what is now Montana. They could not boat up these large waterfalls. The explorers used wheels and axles to pull their boats and supplies on the shore past the falls. This portage took 12 days. Large hail and cold rain fell. Later, the sun was hot. The air was thick with mosquitoes.

On July 27, 1805, the Corps reached the headwaters of the Missouri River. Lewis and a few men left their boats and climbed to the top of the Continental Divide. The Continental Divide is a line that separates east from west in North America. The explorers were disappointed to see more high, snow-covered mountains to the west. They expected the next waterway, the Columbia River, to be about half a day away. But the trip was much farther than that. Still, the Corps of Discovery remained positive.

Sacagawea's people, the Shoshone, lived in the Bitterroot Range of the Rocky Mountains and had horses that Lewis and Clark wanted. Lewis and a few men traveled ahead. He talked to Chief Cameahwait (cah-MEE-ah-wayt) by sign language and told him that a Shoshone woman who could translate was coming with Clark's party. The Corps discovered that Cameahwait was Sacagawea's brother when she arrived with the rest of the group on August 13, 1805. After Sacagawea talked to Cameahwait, he promised to help the expedition.

Lewis and Clark gave the Shoshones food. The explorers brought several dried squashes from the Mandans. Lewis gave the dried squashes to Cameahwait. Cameahwait had the squashes boiled and as Lewis reported "…declared them to be the best thing he had ever tasted except sugar, a small lump of which it seems his sister Sah-cah-gar Wea [Sacagawea] had given him." Lewis also cooked a meal of boiled corn and beans for the Shoshones.

Lewis and Clark reached the Missouri River headwaters at Three Forks, Montana. From there, they could see the Tobacco Root range of the Rocky Mountains.

"…I reflected on the difficulties which this snowey barrier would most probably throw in my way…but as I have always held it a crime to anticipate evils I will believe it a good comfortable road until I am compelled to beleive differently."

—Meriwether Lewis, when first gazing on the Rocky Mountains, May 26, 1805

The Corps of Discovery paved the way for other explorers. In 1833, Karl Bodmer traveled up the Missouri and painted scenes such as this riverside camp.

Corn and Beans with Sunflower Nuts

This recipe calls for cayenne pepper. Cayenne pepper is spicy. If you do not like spicy food, add just a pinch between your thumb and forefinger.

Ingredients

¼ cup butter or margarine
1 cup canned black beans
2 cups canned and drained (or frozen and thawed) whole kernel corn
¾ cup water
⅛ teaspoon salt
⅛ teaspoon ground black pepper
⅛ teaspoon ground red (cayenne) pepper
½ cup unsalted shelled sunflower nuts

Equipment

large saucepan or electric skillet
can opener
colander
wooden spoon
liquid measuring cup
dry-ingredient measuring cups
measuring spoons

1. In large saucepan, melt ¼ cup butter over medium heat.
2. Drain and rinse 1 cup black beans.
3. Add beans and 2 cups corn to saucepan. Cook about 5 minutes.
4. Stir in ¾ cup water, ⅛ teaspoon salt, ⅛ teaspoon pepper, and ⅛ teaspoon red pepper. Bring to a boil over medium heat.
5. Reduce heat to low. Cook about 20 minutes.
6. Stir in ½ cup sunflower nuts and serve.

Makes 6 servings.

Crossing the Bitterroot Range

Lewis was eager to travel over the Bitterroot Range before winter snow fell. The explorers first needed to trade with the Shoshone people for supplies. Cameahwait demanded that Lewis and Clark trade pistols, knives, and bullets for horses. Cameahwait traded 29 horses and a mule to the Corps and allowed two of his people, Old Toby and his son, to travel with the Corps as guides.

In early September 1805, the Corps started the difficult climb up the mountains. The temperature dropped below freezing at night. Hunting was poor. The group ate the last of the salt pork. The explorers missed the buffalo, geese, and other wild game they had hunted on the plains. Without much to eat, many of the men became ill.

Clark carved his signature into a rock formation that he named Pompey's Pillar. Pompey's Pillar is near Billings, Montana.

24

Smoked Salmon Soup

The Corps of Discovery probably would have cooked salmon over a fire, and would not have had vegetables to add to the soup. Their soup would have tasted quite bland. Today, you can make a better-tasting soup with more ingredients.

Ingredients
3 cups canned chicken broth
¼ pound smoked salmon
½ cup green onion (about 4 green onions)
⅓ cup watercress
⅛ teaspoon salt
⅛ teaspoon ground black pepper

Equipment
cutting board
sharp knife
dry-ingredient measuring cups
large saucepan
liquid measuring cup
measuring spoons
wooden spoon

1. Remove skin from salmon. Break salmon into medium chunks.
2. Wash green onions. Trim ends. Cut enough green onions into small slices to fill ½ cup.
3. In saucepan, combine 3 cups broth, salmon, and ½ cup onions. Bring to boil.
4. Reduce heat to low. Cover.
5. Cook for 15 minutes.
6. Wash watercress. Remove stems and trim ends. Measure ⅓ cup trimmed leaves.
7. Add ⅓ cup watercress, ⅛ teaspoon salt, and ⅛ teaspoon pepper to saucepan. Cook another 2 or 3 minutes.

Makes 6 to 8 servings.

Crossing the Bitterroot Range was a challenge for the Corps. Lolo Peak, pictured here, was just one of many tall peaks that the explorers encountered.

The explorers still had supplies of portable soup. For one evening meal, they ate portable soup mixed with water and a little bear's grease. Another day, they killed a colt for their meal. After one wrong turn and 11 hard days of climbing, the Corps and their guides reached the other side of the Bitterroot Range.

They met the Nez Perce on the west side of the Bitterroot Range. These American Indians gave the Corps food. The men welcomed the dried salmon and camas roots that the Nez Perce gave them. But the Corps was not used to this type of food, and many of the men became ill.

Making Maps

One of the most important outcomes of the Lewis and Clark expedition was the new maps that Clark drew. They were the most accurate maps available of the area at the time.

Clark was an excellent mapmaker, although he had no formal training in this area. As the explorers traveled, Clark took compass readings, estimated distances, and made sketches at every riverbend. He later transferred these readings and sketches onto larger maps. Clark completed his initial map readings of the West at Fort Clatsop in the winter of 1806. The original map was 4 feet (1.2 meters) wide. Clark finished the map in 1810 after he and Lewis returned from the expedition.

Clark's map documented the Corps' geographical discoveries. The map showed no direct river route to the Pacific Ocean as Jefferson had hoped. The Corps also had found that the Rocky Mountains were much larger than Americans and Europeans originally thought. The Rocky Mountains separated the Missouri River and the Columbia River systems.

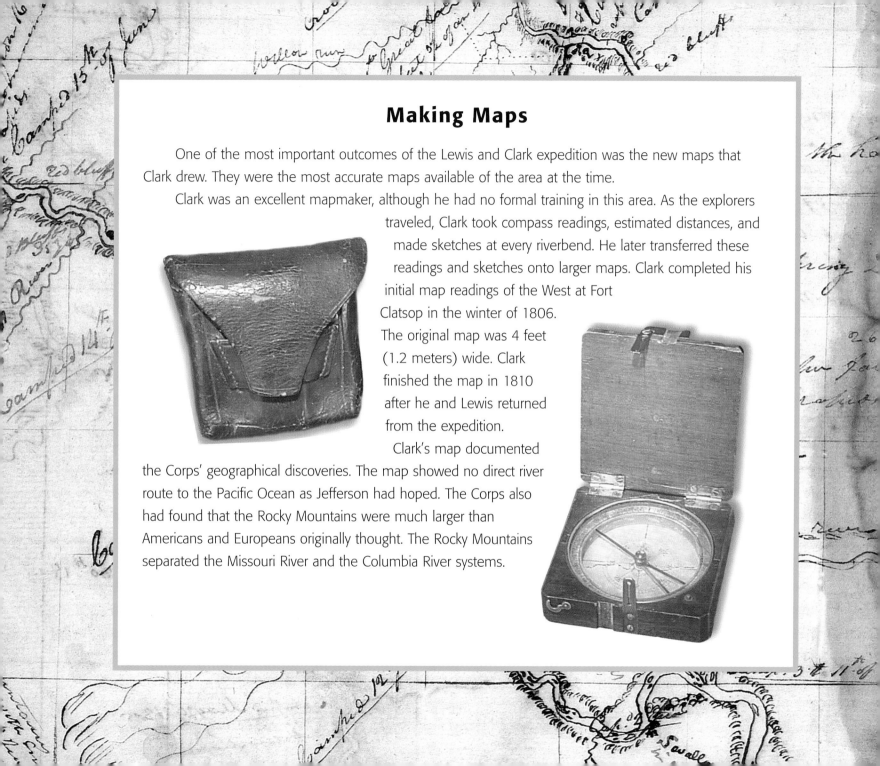

Fort Clatsop near the Pacific Ocean

The explorers paddled downstream from the area north of where present-day Idaho, Washington, and Oregon meet. They traveled on the Clearwater, Snake, and Columbia Rivers. On November 15, 1805, the Corps reached its goal. The explorers had traveled all the way to the Pacific Ocean.

The Corps established a winter camp on the coast. They named it Fort Clatsop for the Clatsop Indians who lived nearby. The Corps spent the winter hunting for elk and deer. The explorers built a smokehouse in which to store meat and fish. They sometimes ate soup made from smoked salmon or herring and roots traded from the Indians.

The Corps spent Christmas at Fort Clatsop. They looked forward to going home and having better food. Clark wrote in his journal on December 25, 1805, "…our Diner [dinner] concisted of pore Elk, so much Spoiled that we eate [ate] it thro' mear necessity, Some Spoiled pounded fish and a fiew [few] roots."

During the winter of 1805 to 1806, the Lewis and Clark Expedition made Fort Clatsop their headquarters.

Many members of the Corps wanted salt to season their food. The explorers boiled seawater for nearly one month to collect about 4 bushels (.14 cubic meters) of salt. They used the salt during the winter and on the journey home.

On March 23, 1806, the Corps left Fort Clatsop. Lewis and Clark split up in Montana to explore and report on more of the land. Lewis's party traveled back along the Missouri River. Clark's party traveled along the Yellowstone River. The parties met when they reached the present-day border of Montana and North Dakota, where the rivers flow together.

On the return trip, the Corps traveled as quickly as possible. By September 1806, the explorers were within 150 miles (241 kilometers) of St. Louis. They ran out of food, but they did not want to take the time to hunt. They lived on wild plums for a few days.

On September 23, 1806, the explorers paddled into St. Louis. People were surprised to see them. The Corps had been gone so long that people thought the group was lost.

The Corps had covered about 8,000 miles (13,000 kilometers) in 28 months. Fur trappers, missionaries, and settlers soon followed into the region Lewis and Clark explored. The Corps of Discovery had opened the way to the West.

Simple Meat Soup

The explorers might have used elk or any other wild game in this basic soup, but you may use beef. This recipe takes an hour of pre-preparation.

Ingredients	Equipment
1 medium potato, unpeeled	cutting board
1 pound lean beef or elk	sharp knife
2½ cups water	large saucepan
2 beef bouillon cubes	liquid measuring cup
¼ teaspoon ground black pepper	measuring spoons
	wooden spoon

1. Partially freeze meat for 20 minutes to 1 hour to make slicing easier.
2. Cut beef into ½-inch (12-millimeter) cubes.
3. In saucepan, combine beef, 2½ cups water, 2 bouillon cubes, and ¼ teaspoon black pepper. Bring to boil.
4. Meanwhile, wash one potato and cut into ½-inch cubes.
5. Add potato cubes to saucepan. Cook over low heat 30 to 40 minutes, until soup thickens slightly.

Makes 6 to 7 servings.

Words to Know

corn boiler (KORN BOI-lur)—a tin cup with no handle used as a cup and bowl; explorers and travelers in the early 1800s used corn boilers.

expedition (ek-spuh-DISH-uhn)—a journey made for a specific purpose, such as exploration

hominy (HOHM-i-nee)—hulled corn kernels.

jerky (JURK-ee)—meat or poultry seasoned with spices and dried over low heat

keelboat (KEEL-bote)—a 55-foot (17-meter) long boat with a square sail designed for shallow rivers; keelboats could carry 12 tons (9 metric tons).

lard (LARD)—oil cooked from pork fat

parched corn (PARCHED KORN)—toasted corn, often ground for meal

pirogue (PEE-rohg)—a long, narrow rowboat

portable soup (POR-tuh-buhl SOOP)—a dry or pastelike mixture that, when added to hot water, makes soup

portage (POR-taj)—the route taken when carrying boats and supplies between two waterways

ration (RASH-uhn)—an amount of food issued to each person; food is rationed so the supply does not run out.

tepee (TEE-pee)—a cone-shaped, portable home used by Plains Indians; a tepee is made by wrapping buffalo or other hides around small tree trunks.

territory (TER-uh-tor-ee)—an area of the United States that is not yet a state

To Learn More

Bowen, Andy Russell. *The Back of Beyond: A Story about Lewis and Clark.* Creative Minds Biographies. Minneapolis, Minn.: Carolrhoda, 1996.

Edwards, Judith. *Lewis and Clark's Journey of Discovery in American History.* In American History. Springfield, N.J.: Enslow Publishers, 1999.

Fradin, Dennis B. *Sacagawea: The Journey to the West.* Remarkable Children. Parsippany, N.J.: Silver Press, 1998.

Isaacs, Sally Senzell. *America in the Time of Lewis and Clark: 1801 to 1850.* Des Plaines, Ill.: Heinemann Library, 1998.

Schanzer, Rosalyn. *How We Crossed the West: The Adventures of Lewis & Clark.* Washington, D.C.: National Geographic Society, 1997.

Places to Write and Visit

Fort Clatsop National Memorial
92343 Fort Clatsop Road
Astoria, OR 97103

**Jefferson National Expansion Memorial
and Gateway Arch**
11 North Fourth Street
St. Louis, MO 53102

**Knife River Indian Villages
National Historic Site**
P.O. Box 9
U.S. Highway 31
Stanton, ND 58571

**Lewis and Clark National Historic
Trail Interpretive Center**
4201 Giant Springs Road
P.O. Box 1806
Great Falls, MT 59403

**North Dakota Lewis and Clark
Interpretive Center**
U.S. Highway 83/North Dakota Highway 200A
P.O. Box 607
Washburn, ND 58577

Internet Sites

Discovering Lewis and Clark
http://www.lewis-clark.org

Fort Clatsop National Memorial
http://www.nps.gov/focl

Lewis and Clark Bicentennial Council
http://www.lewisandclark200.org

Lewis and Clark in North Dakota
http://www.ndlewisandclark.com

Lewis and Clark National Historic Trail
http://www.nps.gov/lecl

Lewis and Clark @nationalgeographic.com
http://www.nationalgeographic.com/
features/97/west

**Lewis and Clark Trail—Re-live the Adventure of
the Corps of Discovery**
http://www.lewisandclarktrail.com

Index